In Jenny Grassl's *Magicholia*, spells and figments fly, phrases and lines emerge like islands filled with strange vegetation, and we are transported to a landscape of language, wild and fresh, where a speaker will "… gather loose holes of migration … over kettles of burning land" or where "seas crash so many stairs" and "moon calves into black." Extinction, a looming dread, haunts these poems, even as the language springs, as if by miracle, struck from a rock, renewed. This is pastoral dipped in fire and swelling with song, an immersive experience unlike in any poetry currently popular. This is Grassl's world, unmistakable and riveting.

—JOAN HOULIHAN, *It Isn't a Ghost if It Lives in Your Chest*

In Jenny Grassl's poem, "Spring Landings," a woman contemplates leaping from a high-rise, noting, as she falls, the details of apartments and lives— dogs, houseplants, tenants' sectional sofas. To read *Magicholia* is to plummet. Grassl writes the silk dress of womanhood, pours facets into cloth, brings her speaker to the brink of death, and pulls her back. Deploying associative images and white space on the page, each line is spell casting— "fall into the well/ really just a tear duct/ salt and undrinkable/ inked with all the words/ for trapped… ." These poems push boundaries of contemporary feminist literature and, with a similar unflinching gaze, Grassl is akin to Sexton. *Magicholia* reveals complexities of female identity but this time with views from a 21st-century tower. I invite you, jump.

—ROBERT CARR, *The Heavy of Human Clouds*

Jenny Grassl's *Magicholia* carries us through deserts and constellations, hospital rooms and fairytale forests, with a poetic voice that feels possessed, visionary. In *Magicholia*, "rhinestones replace eyes of mice," dresses speak and leave teeth marks in the skin, stars "weld gold rings to skeletons." Grassl's sonic richness pierces grief and mania, reorders laws of language and logic. These poems are beautiful, weaponized, glittering in darkness.

—MELISSA GINSBURG, *Doll Apollo*

If poetry apprentices all modes of communication, Sublime Disorientation is the telegraph Jenny Grassl's *Magicholia* sends. "*upon a once* I could begin," she writes, convention's reversal and space-age lineation the bookbinding of these poems' days. Her collection narrativizes mental and physical endangerments and the ways one sleight-of-hand a renaissance. The work's titles ("Thousandfurs," "Greens of Every Latched Place," and "Frail House of Booming" among them) cohere into wizardress cord, terra firma's bungee belts nowhere near as durable as Grassl's risks. Whether garbed as confectioner zoologist ("and who wouldn't want to ride a zebra/ creaming with stars") or carpentry phantasm ("in warped dresser drawers of sakes/ keeped with silks// my grave is undertow"), *Magicholia* materializes "on velvet lapels," Grassl our ascending seamstress.

—JON RICCIO, *Agoreography*

MAGICHOLIA

MAGICHOLIA

POEMS

JENNY GRASSL

ʒ

THREE: A TAOS PRESS

First U.S. edition 2024

Book Design & Typesetting: Lesley Cox, FEEL Design Associates, Taos, NM

Press Logo Design: William Watson, Castro Watson, New York, NY

Front Cover & Interior Artworks, Woodcut/Illustration: Jenny Grassl, Cambridge, MA

Author's Photograph: Jorg Meyer Photography, New York, NY

Text Typeset In: Elmhurst

Printed in the United States of America by Cottrell Printing Company

ISBN: 979-8-9905027-0-3

THREE: A TAOS PRESS

P.O. Box 370627

Denver, CO 80237

10 9 8 7 6 5 4 3 2 1

With loving gratitude, I dedicate *Magicholia* to my husband, Anton Grassl,

and to my children, Isabel Crist and Leo Grassl.

Contents

III. HYSTERIA

IV. THE WELL

This is a love letter to a nightmare

—LEONORA CARRINGTON

I.

DRESSED TO FILL

Meme Mori

                                    too tiny
                                          this model this
                                                 poetry-
                                                       chipped
                         naked lady
                                this embryoid
                                specked rue
                                                       for the moment's rare luster

breath rewound
from all breaths' throstle— sprung-
                                time-
                                traveled
                                faster than light-
                                er than air-
                                borne-
                                again

                                past the red star Antares
last words skidded
                         onto chroma-slid slick
                         muffed in a high-mown cloud

                                black oil shone
                                over the eye of God
                                a fine iridescent brine

                                       I held—
                                       loved ones—
                                       algae bloomed in the planets

A Landfill Dress Mourns

let me tell you the desert in my off-the-shoulder slink—
              velvet yellow she wore me
cat-lazed between her breasts
                                       stalking wild at waist   never
                      thinking of abandonment or soft

            descent from tailor's ham to graveyard junk

        sundown pleating limoncello swish
                what could go wrong except flesh   and a man
                   who loves cloth more

I am all that is left   a dress rushed to ships bound for Chile

                                   dumped where vultures wing slant
                 peck in polyester looking for meat
                   talons tearing buttonholes   portals to saints
        the fragrance of a vamp in death

his tie and cummerbund twist
among legs not here
only stockings

        ripped from her on a first date

ribbons connect the corset of Atacama Desert stars

           who holds a dipper to Andromeda in chains—
           is it half full— the cloth-choked Earth

I lie down with long viridian coats
peeled leaves in a solitude of sand

        this xeric place once throbbed
        air plants   cinching water
        out of ocean fog   lizards hatching

    she was his first murder

  how did rhinestones replace eyes of mice
        no seeds left   they starve
    biting only buttons down my back

this mountain heart heats in sun
           combusts

   my caterwaul   the all-compressed flame

used humors summon robes of angels
hear soughing dunes tell
a whole domain   nature thriving
in a lack of rain   buried alive
each dress like me to blame

Figments

if I were Venus would you ferry me in white

                              bridal foam on a jellyfish

all the girls kept by their churches

                              my T-shirt labeled with China speaks black and white

allegiance to a split rock   Pilgrim or Peter

I live in a house caught with lobster

                and crab of Cancer

condemned in a shaft of light   I blaze

                              a stone golded at my feet   nearly liquid

its mouth open

                                        comber of pretty things

                                        would you find mine on sand

when I am done—

listening shell or a half-hinged

I am tired of the company of stones

waves where I am not

Venus eased by falling flowers

deliver who I am

Earth blamed

like flesh of the scallop

Solo

what good can come of my hair

a follicle ramshackle luck

my scalp aches to be petted like a dog

when I was too young to talk

my father stroked my head

he did not see me at all

coupling myself to a night train

to be seen you can be loved

please do not see me in hospital slippers

dishabille   or spitting

out margarine-buttered white bread

my blood in the inkblot

orbited by a psychiatrist's gold ring

it was my own legal signature

let me through the locked doors

from the crown of my hair

        tears fountain up

        fall to cool the drying

dying earth   O planet

        disrobing   wild-eyed after wildfire

                who will care for your head

where is your mother   where is mine

        to braid your steaming weeds

        and my unkempt

into ornament and talisman

        deflecting punishment

when you open your mouth

        every flowering

Lips

one involuntary eye swiveled to her mouth

candy welling scarlet

when he bit

was it reprieve

the unmasking

artifice he loved   lipstick lick by lick

a custody— soft heat mastering

her allure   clot and pink kissed away   to the shivering

one time she left lips   speaking in tongues on the countertop

refusing their open
and close   no gloss

for melancholia   blood money—   lips bought her—

brought her back to the world

despite their failed cover   telling a story everyone wanted to believe

Framed Edge of Forest

        heavy with gold
           a personal hanging
                in pictures I nearly died to imagine

        everyone alive nearly died
           for something   if the love was strange enough
              a fauve fire on a lake of leaves

diminishes in me— kindles

a false burning
Photoshop appears
truer than life's
gradient dawn and the swung
away moon

what did sky's eye of Jupiter

                see of us blinking
I am a palest mint-green coat
a warm rider   bareback

    and who wouldn't want to ride a zebra
        creaming with stars perspiring   over the skyline

a heaven that occurs to me

With Many Pockets

days hungering   the sport

I try birding   cast my net
                of hairline cracks   eat tiny bones

steal smoke I am naked in
a boa curling sky

I gather loose holes of migration

                watch undecided geese fly

repeating the sign for greater than
throats haunt their narrow

                over kettles of burning land

my lean desire borrows an eye-view
bird-wide enough for heaven

when hungriest I want only
a sighting   identifying
for the notebook

                I hollow any feast

eyes pressed to paired obsidian
binoculars turning inward to a boom

                box in the torso   stomach hard

against itself   what checklist yields claw

has there ever been a time when you
were not your usual self and you felt
so good   or has there ever been
a time when you felt hopeless

Tithe

farm neuralgia for praise   undress
for please   angst in the bank

argue sorrows   their interstice lace   worn
like the browned collar of a long-dead aunt

raid the cupboard for ungrateful suns
open a periodic table for the gods to edit

the chemistry— your love   after all
they can toughen the very softness of rocks

wamble in seasick rave   hail
master of the roast   let the pig turn

take me down to blackened catfish dusk
let the lightning bug not expire

in the valleys tracking my palm   dwindle
every coin   flatten the last penny under a train

Pastimes of the Sane: Clayton Chooses a Prime Time Bride

I don't hate Clayton   bachelor unmoved   not breaken
            in oakum skein of harem hair   gloss waven with starry ices

schools of lakemen and lakemaids breath-dangle suspense in T.V. steam
          studio live blue   swim screen with clotten milk

high in silica   pool superhot like you Clayton   in a north
              prone in pixel glam selfie loss licken   I don't hate Clayton

unmarred   unmarried man   girls baiten by battened down boutonniere
          they wanten and they *outen* all their kiss

what lullaby do you fracken on evening's cradle
        your luxum chasms mothers for your children   I don't hate Clayton

thirty women with eggs   *cries echoing*   would you even read
          the caption   your eyes siphon a god— you as victim

not the strappy gown down   cast damsels   Gabby and Rachel   women you narrowen
         the choice to   Rachel crumples on a stair   *happened*   it is written

about this filmed but real grief   your words   it was a show she croven
       didn't she have a plan for loser   *heavy sigh*   your squirm behoven

where were you born   Eureka   *wrong fucking answer* Gabby scoffs
         spitefully bleepen   *it*   Rachel's moment of profundity spaken

at his love news —*I love you both   but her more*   I don't hate Clayton
        Susie is The One— fled brood hen clucken not yet fucken

Blue-Bleak Embers

heart rind twist in a gin fizz

        black honey-slip through the eye

              of golden bees

vision's sloe hole to what I know   upside down righted

        looking wronged

how my sex is like my eye

yet no lid to stop the flesh

        rub of world   not blinking dark

              hungover light fletches no arrow to pierce the wind

and so   I do not struggle

        to leave the bed

           snug cerement

releasing a white deer

        his distances of moor and hunger

           break my brow

fermenting mind with kiss   circling

        death is something you recover from   not like this

           a blizzard buck

guttered rut by candle door

        pictures finish my life behind my back

Hospital Year Voice

hold the crash in dawn mirrors

ladies of the night removing their lips

present naked to Intake

handing out forms with News Gothic bold-face

paper about to lock my shoes to the ward floor

and close my eyes with consent

take skeleton key beneath the vanish

try to open mouth

diamond insomnias wear down to water   kneeling steam

on the lawns of a summer eloping elsewhere

speak privately   numbers—

bullet questions   *4.* means

Horae of the seasons

deadly horsemen

gospels

where changed to why   were you born

                              June whites and rare meat ransom

              feathers stuck in my lace

I am bride of the asylum brought to be shamed

              in a document

                              I am lost in their mail   in the small of their backstories

why are you on this side of your decisions

                    on the Fourth of July

              my signature is the wrong answer

Thousandfurs

cloaked in the wolf hour/ I fold a solar system of dresses into a nutshell/ hide from my father in a malt barrel tree/ leaking radium and rye/ he would wed me/ likeness of my dead mother/ yellow hair   woe in the oak/ *upon a once* I could begin/ reaching longgold time ago/ landing only with leachate/ my father whiskered crayfish-strange/ he will wreck the forest buck and grub   each threaded root/ leaving a strontium run-off kill/ can I care about blue loam when thrall is fill/ my tattoos rant/ skin a cursive tome of tiny truths/ inked in walnut stain/ drips dyeing   a disguise/ my mother would have fed me prince and silence/ writ large   my words grow lace armor/ I broadcast fire   spells along limbs/ clamor for face/ how easily I facet an infinite

Twinned

slayer and slain   souls forest in all the dressed-to-kill

hound barking up the wrong frill   she   milk bog child

he   her blood booted taker   rosewood violin song drains

sap into its tree   her father's heartbeat   slow tow of an acre

for himself   he   knotted to a bough   slips taut   his dangle

circling her empty slipper shame   stag beetle   chews her name

deep   and young   into oak   limb from limb   her live

buried breath turns its afterleaf   gold   welded to his hunt   he

double crossing   a river waging   above ground she may

have died differently   her soul still paired with him like the first

time   she was murdered   his table place setting   engine die

and car door slam   smoke smell leather and sweat of wood

his chair soaked with sins of the fathers   their axes

II.
MAGIC

Morozko (The Frost King) Asks, Are You Warm Child?

The freezing girl answers using a dictionary, and for lying, she is rewarded with furs and jewels.

1.

I am fine

fyne—

free from dross or alloy

something you owe

I am finished   at the end

and contain a given percent of pure

I am not turbid

I am absolute

and in good health

of immaterial things   say I am elevated

I consist of filaments or slender threads

very small bulk

attenuated   rare

I cut   a small margin

of a ship's pretty bow or a tool

appearing in small print

with delicate perception

artful cunning

… and dandy

I am often used ironically

remarkably good looking

am weather in which the sky is bright

highly showy in dress

my writing is affectedly ornate

also I am what is said of a good woman—

to make little   thin

to break   into particles

2.

unzipped from my skin/ my dress leaves teeth marks/ his gift of fur beneath me bare for lying/ I am supposed to love fur and falsehood/ jewel frosted windows furl his fiended company/ my body to please the shatter of rime/ why tease another skirt from drift/ with lipstick berries in the snow I try/ to draw a bow over a determined point/ on my upper lip to speak the lie— I am warm/ I am strong in my goose bumps/ I know to pretend a melt/ with the frost flowers on his bed/ pooling honey in the sunless sheets/ or else I will eat moss with the reindeer/ I must deny ice diamonds cutting me/ into facets and faults/ my empty shoes point to the exit/ my sisters speak the toads of truth/ *of course I am cold you fool—/* and of course they die

Girls and Ouija Glow the Silence

{1} *Historic Homes Decay After Seizure for a Reservoir*

a letting go

of people we know   we listen for the dead

their small mouths bequeathing the larger kiss

spirits ballooning

like spiders from an egg

too pale for praise

prophecies in millions

the planchette takes

our waking in substitute breath

holding bowls of frost

we ask alphabets winged to war

what are your names

knocking at empty

know bone and lone

between coming flood and eminent domain

flocked ghost-curl

what do stone and rafters mean

{2} *Dam*

we touch our own   twelve years

glassing under   subterranean fish

                we spell and spell   messages outside our will

I am trapped inside my room and the lamp's gone out

                                       let go swimming fingers

cast iron hinges open doors

                                       intimate with reasons

                hands so near each other glide to reach

tale sinking with gabled roofs of a clotted lake

                                              blacken in the wish

daylights gone brown   let go

                                       of felt-hoofed godless

windows riding out of windows

                                       let go the dam never built

eventual bridges birding into night

                       fill the space

{3} Ouija Speaks to Girls

my judder   my halt

dear whole of please   let go

through hole   chipped

sanctuary of face to face

your gaze injures the past

deep home of my spectral hands

mourning and fluent in punishment

shedding caves   hatched wet

in skins   I ice if crush

lean over me

for capture   scintillations

of your hair   copper live wire

to my divining rod

bent in the oculus

to deluge   disputing silence

know that under

I am vowel erect   an I spelled

with sword thrust deciding

earth and sky   a kind of burial

I leave you in knee socks

hands tell me more

what is innocent about greed

umbels of your sweet breath

took houses down to occupy

{4} House

fled key

abandoned wing chair

and cat blur

in shine of a Dutch tile sailing ship

whetstone   hang of linen curtain   let go

the deep in photographs nailing rooms with stare

old newspapers kindle and headline

a woman and her scream in wood grain floor

objects anchor ghosts

mustard seed

on some wispy day

detonate into night

to interrupt stars

beneath draped sheets

{5} Ouija Speaks to Girls as a Woman

hail to vacuums girls cannot fall into

       give back the apple you learned to hate

close as a virus   doubling

         where all the world cloisters

             within you   settle leaves

      in warped dresser drawers of sakes

keeped with silks

                 my grave is undertow   glacier candled

leaving nothing where it was

             let go your bodies in basal slip

        gaze on a turquoise heart   cased in black debris

            I will finally drown

                cups in cupboards

        with thaw   even your skate-scratched ice

melt and love the lake

Tarot for Climate

we trudge our hearten   cuppen the reeken

water   wave our wands sprouten

to restore tree   plunge our swords in cliffs

to letten out sea   pentacles dust an alley

where the dark eyed closen the deck   to thumb

and spark   queen creepen under skin of card

to arid   spoil of waterfall   open the way

with number   and reign   answer rock

clamoring   sovereign clocked   keep

no destination from the fork   in tongued

sands thirsten   beauty's stumbling frock

lipped by ocean   far from unturned outcome

promising some shimmy   too shine   O clime

Conserves

September is what I am cooking in the demon pot of suns   so less and less

of blue   skies spoiled in the grape   loosed   vine and thread   gone

gobbledygook   attached to witch light of July   corkscrew   limbed acrobat

of seeking   woody now   filament   monument to my own falling   I could save

our vacation in greener leaves with vinegar   toss the spider in the eaves

dislodge ghouls from cottage rooms   funnel them into jars to preserve their sight

like the frog clear-eyed in his brine   cured   so we can poke and name his parts

names for it all melancholia   this purpling browse   the ripe smell in the house

Mania Diary: Plumed

fenghuang   a foreshadow   she/

he

foreign bird to my tongue   thick with spell

out of flood crest   crate oranges and shoes   brown river lifts

cockscomb   a long tail

vermilion cut from night-letting sun

when I kiss from a hurt

when will I resemble

in a quarter of heaven

an eavesdrop

on irregular valleys

mountains   looking for error

ranging inside my alembic fire

everlasting fermata

over mania dawn

the pentatonic poised to weep

this   a change song

and the bird's wide tune through hemlocks

wing curve

an arranging of noise

breaking wedding bells

golden in the ear

between salt peaks of an old medicine

sighting *fenghuang* is a sign from a great height

I am porous for signs landing inside me

amulet ambulant to chime   every cashier's ring with *fenghuang*

every logo an old story   déjà vu of the he/ she bird   new claim

a hemp dress hangs with the usefulness of a noose

why kick the chair away   a new set of notes

see the old body torque-breasted in the talons

dropped in the atria of a divided

Debacle Web

what do I lose

          at the unburdening

                            I silk

an arc

                      umbilical cord to fasten

                         rain   my hands cup

                      sibilance   silver

whisper droplet-knit

                      repair the net   *regold*   *twist with noonsong*

                      on the hospital steps

shelter in ballroom   cheek on velvet lapels

sanctum   veil   the masked nuptial

wayfaring ox pulls breath from sleep

a bridge of grass sewn to Mars

arachnid web is thought   spiderlings truss pieces of mind

between dirt crumbs   anchored

at rock and root

can survivors weave havoc with shine

ladder sequined to a meadow

Shae

Dear J—
copper mine makes gangrene

I see you   teen face aged and twitched
in your hospital rain

tunnels wake the dead of England in fields

please return my burn
in your daily bowl

our eyes hunger for ruffed grouse   northern flicker
(their Audubon halt in nervous flight   tract houses circle
warships around our island corn   (Fear has a smell of wilderness

(lunch money and gym class stolen from God

lights walking

you know it is never enough
why do you pretend
I want to be a freshet freed
you interrupt star clutter   moon friend
it grows with voyage
write it in your food of me
my dog is a spirit from the southern sky

I give you all the trees and a doors and windows truck
to save us from hearses   when I see you suited under flowers
we unwrap the fast food cow alive again

(fifty moonlit gulls make a flag over me

(all my salt delivered in a pile

(peals of lovekeep

(your black dress someone's vernal pool

you should go home now   stop talking to the dead

is the body all we can manage for a resurrection
            there is wing in a stone
                    (a magicholia
                        Your Friend Ringing— S

III.
(HYSTERIA
(

Snow White in the Dolomite Mountains

I fall new/ fever ruby into the mine of a hungry mountain/ sacrificed virgin   swallowed by the Queen of Dolomite/ my cheeks slurred in her cliffs   capture of sunset nightly/ rock trapping life ancient and sea/ I see the tracks back   fossils/ every shadow requires favor// in my grave cave the Fire Salamander whitens and grows dragon-high/ why did he sway me into an asphyxiate-blue waltz/ our steps in the airless// miners find me   dead/ smitten they preserve my body/ a glass coffin far above the tree line/ I lie like a moth de-fluttered closure sewn by a prince/ whipstitched eyelash and wing/ he hauls me to his castle/ keeps my child corpse close to him for many drenches of sun exhumed by moon// once I cough waking/ undoing his love spell/ he hurries me back to cloud/ does he know if I live again I will one day weather   overcast// snow mortal as bone   alone I open the pearl-dusk lid/ eclipse of white grit/ blackening the peaks/ my crow craw hair ravenous/ gone avalanche gray

Autumn Yard Swept Into the Collector's Box

I know darkling/ jewel/ rain

beetle kinds   birds eat names
                from the panic grass
cats eat science
                but really is it personal

I roll the ball of a pen
across a page of unseen

                taxonomy   have I distempered

the larger winds waiting
for glitter of coleoptera in scarlet branches

                abrupt wings glassine
                depart along a fold   why

do I grip grail and miss
the rail   why not hold on to

only the body   and the built world
classify what crushes— magic

                holding the physical   a beauty you can say
                in numbers

what is staring and eavesdropping
which eaves   and how do they drop

                    listening in on birds to correct
in hydrangea heads of throng

I wet with lips and tongue

each day with feline care
and an ache for what it cost

                    the cotton under glass beds my bell-
worn persona   no death freeing me

the ears' channels fuzz

every season of burnish flouncing away
to disenchant   for a cycle of the sun

Spell For Rescue in a Catastrophe—
Be Prepared, Be Coifed

Anthropocene alive you are
Because your mirror labored
Riddle of camisole crink
Angled hairline wave

Command now shimmer
Arms of sequined dew
Damask georgette moire
Albumen thickened pearls
Bejewel your strong thigh lambs
Running from tundra wolves
Avoid no man's triage of women

Angel-fake   be lemon-haired
Bewitch suitors' bricolage tastes
Rescue likely in haute couture
Accents androgyne and thin

Crux of your candor slender heeled
Astral shift dress a silver sliver
Drunk on opera silk   manage
Aplomb in planet's dive
Borage-blinked eye shadow blued
Revise the central Haul of Shame
After-party landfill shoes

Briar Rose as Hysteric at the End of the World

will not wick a rose unto June/ desire's fossil plants and animals slick

spill city/ how many skies steam over triple-deckers and choking eglantine/ only thorned

kingdom ajar/ keenest hawk elegy/ lamp left on hot and useless/ to wake a hundred years

and then/ lie with the prince deeper than clothes/ master the century of addled blue/

unbidden magic/ sleep's new insomniac dawn/ princess lush proclaiming ash/ loud

tongue/ bramble pierced/ to tell/ to bawl the over

Wandering Womb as Cause of Hysteria

Earth's wolf not fixed in her roams

uterus problem doctors say   such furious

weather   feral seas   she moves

galaxy through muse and murder

near extinction   moon calves into black

angle of womb too low

to cure   hellebore

mint and laudanum raise the golden pear

organ of menarche   mother and crone

good God from where

doctors offer her themselves

healing sex   smelling salts   decoctions

of tamarind   barley   cassia pulp and lime

with belladonna   leeches

try to freeze north and south

between teeth and legs

be maenad in wine

sleep with Saturn

all willing

sickness is remedy

pleases

so doctors think clitoridectomy

women help her   musk oil and lemon melissa

     men do of course want to help   wildfire

         and exorcism   doctors fumigate the vagina

kept in sky hospital

       treatment switched to sex stanch

and death sentence   her witchery blamed

for planet fever   floods and dying crops

     how pure Mars must be with only a history

     dark with water   making war   dust

       how to find swing

         of planetary mood

she woken by lantern every time eyes close

at night as orbit bed check

       in a euthanizing lake the lost wolf

Hysteria Medicine

   — propped up a diagnosis
sunspot plumes
blotto
benign
      note to self— fill ~~daily~~ boxes with correct ~~pills & gratitude~~
With Love and   Gratitude— *RX# please leave your name and phone #*
I should carry you Aripiprazole in a lacquered pillbox in a faux zebra purse I
would race medicine heady-bright through this age of reason with devil-may-care
and trail mix nuts raisins and you in a faux zebra purse

      Dear Aripiprazole— Preventer of Manic Episodes—
why do you cause the best manic episodes and why don't I mind your fail
snow-during-advent medicine buxom Disneyland and diamond-spurred cowboy
medicine you accrue to me like a circle of friends with mass appeal fashion medicine
full flounce Medicine Becoming Partly Windy After a Swelter— Hallelujah
whiskey to a parched sailor medicine on the dance floor on Donner and Blitzen
a whole museum of fine fine arts   reality TV with me the laughing star
popcorn medicine chicken-fried outright outlandish medicine me delivered from
clichés and evil   pitter-patter of little pill feet   wonderland contraband
counter-cultural medicine pre-destiny medicine   high Catholic mass medicine
quack country doctor medicine o fast car and big house medicine   lipstick on
the mirror for you medicine kudos and kilted dancers and glass bowls of guppies and
a few of my Rogers and Hammerstein Favorite Things   and lo favored flavor your
resume is scant— how provocative   but you're hired for one mired in a past of
false admirers— Zyprexa etcetera   you require only my daily doting dosing
and unbelievably positive outlook

With Love in Paradoxical Reaction,
Your fan—

End Song

mostly she worries about ka

surviving after death

condemned or elated

to witness the slow repeal of the body

she speaks only

of a washing and lapping inside

spirit against the ribs

a kind accompanying   alive

but the expiring earth may keep a soul and

where shall it live

she sees a blue place

in the warm and cool of telescoped stars

in her phone   aroused billions of light years ago

sparking in a pocket of space   a planet begins in galaxy foreplay

a heat wave bobble of flowering

the stars shall weld gold rings to skeletons   sunflowers to their skies

each apocalypse to a genesis

IV.
THE WELL

The Manic Little Match Girl Turns Suicidal

she uses all the light/ her matches struck/ a handheld herd of fire running to spread sky/ spirits look down   blinded/ skein-trapped wildcats tangling into towns/ whole gapes of ocean filling with scorched ships/ her fleet of dreams does not keep her alive/ but does help her to die/ she sells no match/ her father's lamp burns down for her return/ for counting coins or lashes/ alone with a snowflake she refuses to cry/ inside her silence rises/ her throat a foreign body turns/ into him   turning on her/ she chooses bone in a glove of ice/ curled on the street/ her grandmother beloved   blue in the last flame /// strike by strike we use all the light/ far below the night jet wing/ we watch from the window at 30,000 feet   a meadow/ a violet-thick fluorescence/ factories webbing yellow across the land/ luminous highways vining to an infinite rose/ the houses look so warm/ we were so cold   we lit the dark/ but now at end we must choose/ the carbon printing foot brought down hard upon the land/ our hair on fire or else ice   an age

Space Moth   Bipolar Nebula

I am of two stars

        collapsed envelope of dust and gas

open and close moth

        the lover half

metamorphic ache   a hanging   and wet

               +++

my center cannot choose

        I hold the kiss   proboscis drinking galaxy tears

compound eye borrows

               moldered apple

               cold bile

      even flowers are skull cap and swamp candles

O loss I go spare   in dress of dawn char

+++

of the maniacal roving madness—

aflirt   skirted sails fill and empty

I want to sleep with all the victors of the new world

confect an ease

lay many eggs

night gowned knocking at clock bright

+++

sun up all night   chain-reactive lace

high on holes of design and chewed wool

flowers are fatal   and I don't care

if everything means—   cascading—   I cannot—

smallest done thing destroys

I radiate ragged   death-tease   flutter of   mine

Spring Landings

ship full sail

on the way to his desert

seas crash so many stairs

all the inamoratas

skirts floating up

in the hull and mouth   sand

I am mirage to serve

a hoped quench

scrapes sky

reaches pyre

of another clever eye

no sign not to take the elevator in case of brimstone

on the arm of wrong

door held

roof garden

julienned in late light

city bowing with earth's curve

calling home

to mind

higher rooms   risk of vacancy

the edge

a wake of scarves

traveling musk   I could be cloud

tower oversleeping midnight

will a silk dress soften any fall

trailing lights

unstrung amaranth   and potted fig invite

one step from ledge to Lethe

I could choose

plummet by

windows

of wolfhounds

sectional sofas

sansevieria

and a barque in a bottle's lost century

dropping far

whose lives these are

would pass before my eyes

sidewalk pores widen   want me

               for nightfallen entry   knife of the sun

when did lesser celandine land here

                    blooms

            lemon   rivering

         sugar and grit kissed

           in forgetfulness

bees close flowers along day's end

Peak and Trough

prone to wave a hand at melancholy

my arm branching   a wand

olive wood   with silver bangle

conductive

zaps the lapsed

back to bleed

back to majolica

and lemons

mattering

after mottling

red and magenta of afternoon

in summer

macular loss of hue

like mulberry

leavings of birds bleaching in sun

why do sunspots obscure entry into the cool house

of dog sleep rising

why had I not seen

how moss gathers on a rolling   rollicking meteor

landed in this room called living

Suicide Watch

                 the bed is dy   in   g

sleep deprive   d   wind   in g sheet welter—merec   loud

change from rabbit   to rabbit in mouth

                      of
            fox   ) the night body

night shift's prey

                              hospital check   ed   e   very quarter hour

      flashlight

           cone clawed from chest rise
      to eyelid try   ing   to flicker dream—

checkmate—   woke   n people die

           a know   n   torture   watch

                for every single ray on the cross   ed-out dark

eye   s   tar vanish   radial flame

                                        crowds retina with finch murmur

dozens gilt and fleck   ed

                    flashing   arc swings forthe next   bed

sweat   f o g   of goddess glare   g oldening her brass children

            upside down in the eye   voyeurs

                    murder   (i) ng   say I   took my own

                                        watch me watch

                        them

The Quiet Room

Why do you think you were put in the Quiet Room?

) because on divot duggen from square lawn I camen

turf abunden with fleshly

grub and crispen ones creepen   crept to fly   wingen July

any other reason

the room for quieten

of hallway   my remove

help smoothen shuffle of other

ruin

((the sound I won't maken   lone fell

my pelt long strippen   necklace and belt

)))hospital locken))))

walls padden before I camen

ceiling pressen down   floor risening

when lock clicken aftershove   of course throw self at door   out

wanten   if gaven up they will offern only proper noise   droppen pill into paper

cup   a water drinken taint   soft moon of easier

patients' moan   (

                                                              it is flight I sky in fiberboard

                              vent blown   white noise of wings   (keepen beating

                                                              my elbow without fatten or sinew

                    vein wrappen bone I've scathen

my dappling eye rubben sore

              a regatta of spots hiden the dead seen air

                              (((((((

              how long will I been in here)))))))))

                                                              room herein—

                                                              quiet bricken

                                                              mortal mortarn

                                                  the ones lacken family longer stayn

fear is not louden with me usual

howl is not louden with me usual

cry is quieten

they daylong asken   staff they mocken

feeling better   ¿?   feeling better

widening pore to pour

a drowning

this room with no bed no chair

to flailen   I butterfly in churchen hands

flittering   away

a joyful noise

so

unquieten

in the ledgers

of locken

Frail House of Booming

madness has its dramatis personae
        take Witch of Wax   and Queen of Wane

gather nature's undersides   all smoke-fleshed bellies
        the compost crawl   and dustbowl's flatulent sky

take gypsy caterpillar stickiness   failing at silk
        or barbed wheels loose— snow edginess

wild horse dressage and shed skin stumble
        build all unto plush   a purple veined

kiss your melancholies can feel
        irises   to cup and bury   pollen labored bees

snowflakes fit bright onto a land of soot
        my mind lit   somehow unruly

makes last burn turn into new grass   new pine
        and I exchange my skeleton for meat

slender protagonist   worm for robin
                robin for my spring

Magicholia

        fall into the well

really just a tear duct   salt and undrinkable

        inked with all the words

                for trapped   drowning

        ultramarine no name for the bruise

            tube of melancholy

        odoring far down   redder

                sea of magma dawn   blood and my stage

        fright birth   I am my mother's

crescendo in lava rain

        she   so close to a star

and I   tumbled from the locked-dark side of her planet

        she bows to applause

            they place me in her distant arms

        the 'o' of *hello* not rising   no bubble

no ruby from an igneous

my grief a lantern to find burnt things

how can I speak of speech

                        I land at births of my own

children pushing apart my hips

        crack me into two mothers

                   my dark child reaches

        is this not joy

                  how much more I have

        to lose   relict species of grief join down here—

a canceled marrying   an exile of myself as favored daughter—

        baring their teeth   just to go on

in this fathomless drop   hold

                the ocean

shark fins cutting their leather above the waves

a marsh slips into the well

        braid the reedy hay for a ladder to climb

dragging animal glut and gland

                    sac of the sweet   clam and yellow bittern

        and the horribles   white truck with woman

           corpse at the wheel

        hydra and skunk ape   seeking

        an ark   I refuse no kind

                                   a red bird glides beside me

                 flame flower

smelling of iron and spice

                                to wipe the surface mirror

fogged with ancestral

                 Narcissus

                       at the rim of the wound   find a tree

                       a snake whispers   *eat*

                             share   you already know

                             your wellspring

                       what you have in tow

Greens of Every Latched Place

our last-minute dead carousing
wolves and passerines foundering

once bolted in   kept only by sighs
of habit   angels eased heaven's lock

to latch   my double espresso steams a swan
with broken wing   down to grounds

bottom of the cup losing curves
to chaos and farther weather

lindens wait for little clapper fruits
to harden their seed and ring

tolling grand and spent perfume
I pressed a fog once between my knees

to rain for you   rosemary or wine
tang of storms and dulcets

every moment is an extinction
the crosswind of spirit drinking loam

trying on frond and green bond
all the graffiti famished

the book signing the hand
skin racing into its own summer

ink pleasures deep
                    tagging the body with yours

Notes

The Seventh Horse and Other Tales, Plume, New York, NY, 1988 is the source of the Leonora Carrington quotation. Carrington was a British-born surrealist painter and writer who lived mostly in Mexico. She was born in 1917 and died in 2011.

The definitions for "fine" in **"Morozco (The Frost King) Asks, *Are You Warm Child?*"** are loosely taken from *The Oxford English Dictionary*, Second Edition, prepared by J. A. Simpson and E.S.C. Weiner; reprinted 1994, Oxford University Press, Oxford, U.K.

The dam referred to in the poem **"Girls And Ouija Glow The Silence"** is the Evansburg Dam. It was part of a project in Pennsylvania to flood an historic town and surrounding countryside to create a reservoir. Residents were forced to leave their homes under the law of eminent domain, allowing government seizure of property. The houses stood empty for years and decayed to ruin as the project lagged and was ultimately canceled.

"Briar Rose" is the name of the Grimm brothers' story of "Sleeping Beauty."

Ka appears in **"End Song,"** a word from ancient Egyptian religion referring to one aspect of the soul. The exact meaning is controversial, but it is sometimes the divine spirit of a person that can live in a picture or statue.

"Wandering Womb As Cause Of Hysteria" is about the belief that the wrong position of the womb in a woman's body causes hysteria. This idea is first found in Egypt in 1900 B.C. and persisted well into the 19th century. Many cures including sex, sex repression, poison, and mutilation were given to hysterical women.

I use the term "paradoxical reaction" in the poem **"Hysteria Medicine."** In this poem, it refers to the increase in a bipolar patient's mania when the medicine is intended to diminish or cure the mania.

The title **"Blue-Bleak Embers"** is taken from a line in a poem of Gerard Manley Hopkins, in "Windhover," *Poems of Gerard Manley Hopkins*, Humphrey Milford, London, United Kingdom, 1918.

Bipolar Nebula, appearing in **"Space Moth   Bipolar Nebula,"** is a celestial nebula created from a central star with two wing-like lobes on either side. As a star nears the end of its life, it pushes the outer layers into space. The matter is funneled to the poles of the star, making a shape like a butterfly. There are theories that the nebulae are created out of binary stars.

"The maniacal roving madness," from my poem **"Space Moth   Bipolar Nebula,"** is taken from Hermann Boerhaave's *Documentary History of Psychiatry*, ed. Charles Goshen, Philosophical Library, New York, 1967, 230.

Taken from the season finale of *Bachelor*, the T.V. series, **"Pastimes Of The Sane: Clayton Chooses A Prime Time Bride"** is based on the real life sorrows of the contending women. The show was filmed in Iceland in 2022.

Robert MacFarland and Sianne Ngai describe the language of shock and grief: "When shocked or grieving we find ourselves able to speak of the experience only in 'thick speech.'"
From anthropocenetransitions.org, kjmcl/wordpress.com, Kenneth McCleod, 4/ 30/ 17, by Karoline Kvellestad Isaksen.cas,oslo.no. Among others, **"Tarot For Climate,"** **"Suicide Watch,"** and **"The Quiet Room"** are poems in thick speech.

Acknowledgments

I gratefully acknowledge the following journals in which these poems first appeared or are forthcoming:

Blaze Vox, a Journal of Voice: "Magicholia," "Debacle Web," and "Thousandfurs"

Inverted Syntax: "Twinned"

Lily Poetry Review: "Pastimes of the Sane: Clayton Chooses a Prime Time Bride"

Ocean State Review: "Figments"

Phantom Drift: "Conserves"

Radar Poetry: Finalist for The Coniston Prize: "Solo," "Meme Mori," "Briar Rose as Hysteric at the End of the World," "Tarot for Climate"

Tupelo Quarterly: "Girls and Ouija Glow the Silence," "A Landfill Dress Mourns," "Hospital Year," and "Frail House of Booming"

Notes of Appreciation

For Anton Grassl, my husband; Isabel Crist and Leo Grassl, my children; to Fay and Powell Lawton, my parents; Pamela Lawton, my sister; and Tom Lawton, my brother. Each member of this family has lived by the belief that the creative life is possible, and for this inspiration and support, I am grateful.

For my Boston area poetry companions: Gale Batchelder, Kelly DuMar, Julia Thacker, Eve Linn, Ted Clausen, Lisa Kaufman, Catherine Morocco, Judson Evans, Martha McCollough, Eileen Cleary, Robert Carr, Paul Nemser, Aimée Sands, and Eric Braud. For these people and others too numerous to name, gratitude for our friendship and work in poetry.

For my teachers, mentors, workshop and conference leaders: Thomas Daley, Lucie Brock-Broido, Liam Rector, David Lehman, Joan Houlihan, Kristina Marie Darling, Jeffrey Levine, and Dick Lebowitz: I thank you for accompanying me with your wisdom on this journey.

For Jorg Meyer and his excellent photographic vision in creating my author photograph, my appreciation.

For friendship and support I especially appreciate: Wendy and John Berger, Melanie Hedlund, Louise Berliner, Jean Hermann, Eileen Burke, Mary Ann Williams, and Tamara Krendel.

For a sure and inspired hand, and for believing in *Magicholia,* I thank Andrea Watson, editor of 3: A Taos Press. I also am thankful for the treasure of all the other 3: A Taos Press books she and the other members of the 3: A Taos Press team have brought into the world. For Lesley Cox, of FEEL Design Associates, my admiration and thanks for the highly original and beautiful design of this book.

About the Author and Artist

Jenny Grassl grew up in Collegeville, Pennsylvania, and now lives in Cambridge, Massachusetts. She received her M.F.A. in poetry from Bennington Writing Seminars and her B.F.A. from Rhode Island School of Design where she majored in photography and also studied painting and drawing. She has published in many poetry journals including *Boston Review, Tupelo Quarterly, Bennington Review, Lana Turner,* and *Ocean State Review,* and her poetry was featured in a *Best American Poetry* blog.

In her work as a visual artist, Jenny has created images with poetry and automatic writing in a variety of media, including photography, collage, painting, printmaking, and sculpture. Presently, she is focused on photography collage.

Jenny has exhibited widely, including at the Joyce Goldstein Gallery, Chatham, New York; Janapa Gallery, New York, New York; The Center for Book and Paper Arts, Chicago, Illinois; Atlantic Works Gallery, Boston, Massachusetts; The Gallery at Atlantic Wharf, Boston, Massachusetts; and Arsenal Center for the Arts, Watertown, Massachusetts.

Combining language and image has been the focus of most of her work, both visual art and poetry. In visual art, Automatic Writing and poetry create the text, offering a shorthand or personal hieroglyphic images. The art and poetry both come out of a love of language, and they speak about human relationships and the realm of myth and magic, in a time of climate change and misogyny.

Also By Three: A Taos Press

Collecting Life: Poets On Objects
Known and Imagined
Madelyn Garner & Andrea Watson

Seven
Sheryl Luna

The Luminosity
Bonnie Rose Marcus

3 A. M.
Phyllis Hotch

Trembling in the Bones:
A Commemorative Issue
Eleanor Swanson

Ears of Corn: Listen
Max Early

Elemental
Bill Brown

Rootwork
Veronica Golos

Farolito
Karen S. Córdova

Godwit
Eva Hooker

The Ledgerbook
William S. Barnes

The Mistress
Catherine Strisik

Library of Small Happiness
Leslie Ullman

Day of Clean Brightness
Jane Lin

Bloodline
Radha Marcum

Hum of Our Blood
Madelyn Garner

Dark Ladies & Other Avatars
Joan Roberta Ryan

The Doctor of Flowers
Rachel Blum

Bird Forgiveness
Melinda Palacio

Turquoise Door
Lauren Camp

The Cairns: New and Selected Poems
Bill Brown

We Are Meant To Carry Water
Tina Carlson, Stella Reed &
Katherine DiBella Seluja

The Unbuttoned Eye
Robert Carr

The Burnings
Gary Worth Moody

Girl
Veronica Golos

Quivira
Karen Kevorkian

godspine
Terri Muuss

Anyone's Son
David Meischen

Vanishes
D E Zuccone

World As Sacred Burning Heart
Jeremy Paden

Abyss & Bridge
Renée Gregorio

Manifold: poetry of mathematics
E R Lutken

M
Dale M. Kushner

Agoreography
Jon Riccio

100 Days
James Navé

Blood Secrets
Anita Rodriguez, Joan Ryan, & Andrea Watson

The Heavy of Human Clouds
Robert Carr

Little Souls and the Selves
Leslie Ullman

Twelve Days From Transfer
Eleanor Kedney

Life Afterlife / A Book of the Hours
Katherine Durham Oldmixon Garza